For release on delivery
9:00 a.m. EDT
September 2, 2010

Statement by

Ben S. Bernanke

Chairman

Board of Governors of the Federal Reserve System

before the

Financial Crisis Inquiry Commission

Washington, D.C.

September 2, 2010

Chairman Angelides, Vice Chairman Thomas, and other members of the Commission, your charge to examine the causes of the recent financial and economic crisis is indeed important. Only by understanding the factors that led to and amplified the crisis can we hope to guard against a repetition.

Appropriately, the problem of too-big-to-fail, and the policies that the government uses to address that problem, will be a particular focus of your forthcoming report and in the hearing today. In my view, the too-big-to-fail issue can best be understood in the broader context of the financial crisis itself. Accordingly, this testimony provides an overview of the factors underlying the crisis, as well as some of the problems that complicated public officials' management of the crisis. Too-big-to-fail financial institutions were both a source (though by no means the only source) of the crisis and among the primary impediments to policymakers' efforts to contain it. As you requested, I will also briefly discuss monetary policy during the period prior to the crisis. Before proceeding, I should state that my testimony reflects my own views and not necessarily those of my colleagues on the Board of Governors of the Federal Reserve System or the Federal Open Market Committee (FOMC).

Triggers of the Crisis

In discussing the causes of the crisis, it is essential to distinguish between triggers (the particular events or factors that touched off the crisis) and vulnerabilities (the structural weaknesses in the financial system and in regulation and supervision that propagated and amplified the initial shocks). Although a number of developments helped trigger the crisis, the most prominent one was the prospect of significant losses on residential mortgage loans to subprime borrowers that became apparent shortly after house prices began to decline. With more than $1 trillion in subprime mortgages outstanding, the potential for losses on these loans was large in absolute terms; however, judged in relation to the size of global financial markets, prospective subprime losses were clearly not large enough on their own to account for the magnitude of the crisis. (Indeed, daily movements in global equity markets not infrequently impose aggregate gains or losses equal to or greater than all the subprime mortgage losses incurred thus far.) Rather, the system's vulnerabilities, together with gaps in the government's crisis-response toolkit, were the principal explanations of why the crisis was so severe and had such devastating effects on the broader economy.

In midsummer 2007, events unfolded that would engender a sea change in money market conditions, triggered by fears of subprime losses that had been growing during the first half of the year. To choose one of several possible key dates, on July 30, 2007, IKB, a medium-sized German bank, announced that in order to meet its obligations, it would be receiving extraordinary support from its government-owned parent and an association of German banks. IKB's problem was that its Rhineland off-balance-sheet vehicle was no longer able to roll over the asset-backed commercial paper (ABCP) it had been issuing in U.S. markets to fund its large portfolio of asset-backed securities. Although none of the securities in the Rhineland portfolio was in default and only some were subprime-related, commercial paper investors had become concerned about IKB's ability to meet its obligations in the event that the securities Rhineland held were downgraded.

Around the same time, other vehicles similar to that of Rhineland were also finding funding rollovers to be more costly and difficult to arrange. These difficulties intensified over subsequent weeks, as investors around the world pulled back funding; indeed, outstanding U.S. ABCP plummeted almost $200 billion in August. The economist Gary Gorton has likened this pullback to a traditional bank run: Lenders in the commercial paper market and other short-term money markets, like depositors in a bank, place the highest value on safety and liquidity.[1] Should the safety of their investments come into question, it is easier and safer to withdraw funds--"run on the bank"--than to invest time and resources to evaluate in detail whether their investment is, in fact, safe. Although subprime mortgages composed only a small part of the portfolios of most structured credit vehicles, cautious lenders pulled back even from those that likely had no exposure to subprime mortgages. The resulting funding pressure was in turn transmitted to major banks that had sponsored or provided funding guarantees to vehicles. Short-term funding in the interbank market became more difficult and costly. Over subsequent quarters, instability in global money markets worsened and posed an increasingly serious threat to the functioning of a range of financial markets and institutions, which in turn constricted the flow of lending to nonfinancial borrowers. Ultimately, the disruptions to a range of financial markets and institutions proved far more damaging than the subprime losses themselves.[2]

Although subprime mortgage losses were the most prominent trigger of the crisis, they were by no means the only one. Another, less well-known triggering event was a "sudden stop" in June 2007 in syndicated lending to large, relatively risky corporate borrowers. Funding for these "leveraged" loans had migrated in recent years from banks to special purpose vehicles; these vehicles funded themselves by issuing collateralized loan obligations (CLOs), a type of asset-backed security. CLOs were purchased by a variety of investors, including ABCP vehicles. At the time, the sudden stop in origination of new syndicated loans was seen by some as a bargaining ploy by lenders seeking higher interest rate spreads, but a side effect was a modest drop in the market prices of outstanding loans, which in turn raised the possibility of downgrades

---

[1] See Gary B. Gorton (2008), "The Panic of 2007," paper presented at "Maintaining Stability in a Changing Financial System," a symposium sponsored by the Federal Reserve Bank of Kansas City, held in Jackson Hole, Wyo., August 21-23; the paper is available at www.kansascityfed.org/publications/research/escp/escp-2008.cfm.
[2] Indeed, in the end, losses on subprime mortgages would not have been nearly so great if vulnerabilities in the financial system had not led to such large adverse effects on economic activity and house prices.

of some CLOs. As in the case of subprime mortgages, the perceived potential losses on leveraged loans in the late summer of 2007 were significant, although not large enough by themselves to threaten global financial stability. But they damaged the confidence of short-term investors and, consequently, the functioning of money markets and the broader financial system.

Other triggers also helped begin the cascade of events that became the crisis. My purpose is not to provide an exhaustive list but to convey that problems that may be individually manageable can set off a crisis when the financial system is sufficiently vulnerable. I turn now to a discussion of some of those vulnerabilities, beginning with those in the private sector.

Vulnerabilities in the Private Sector

As the severity of the crisis has eased over the past year and attention has focused on financial reform, much of the discussion has been about shortcomings of public-sector policies and responses. Those shortcomings were important, and I will return to them shortly. However, many key vulnerabilities were products of private-sector arrangements.

Dependence on Unstable Short-Term Funding

Shadow banks are financial entities other than regulated depository institutions (commercial banks, thrifts, and credit unions) that serve as intermediaries to channel savings into investment. Securitization vehicles, ABCP vehicles, money market funds, investment banks, mortgage companies, and a variety of other entities are part of the shadow banking system. Before the crisis, the shadow banking system had come to play a major role in global finance; with hindsight, we can see that shadow banking was also the source of some key vulnerabilities.

Leading up to the crisis, the shadow banking system, as well as some of the largest global banks, had become dependent on various forms of short-term wholesale funding. Over the past 50 years or so, a number of forms of such funding have emerged, including commercial paper, repurchase agreements (repos), certain kinds of interbank loans, contingent funding commitments (such as commitments that investment banks provided for auction rate securities, used primarily to finance municipalities), and others. In the years immediately before the crisis, some of these forms of funding grew especially rapidly; for example, repo liabilities of U.S. broker dealers increased by 2-1/2 times in the four years before the crisis.

As was illustrated by the ABCP market meltdown discussed earlier, the reliance of shadow banks on short-term uninsured funds made them subject to runs, much as commercial banks and thrift institutions had been exposed to runs prior to the creation of deposit insurance. A run on an individual entity may start with rumors about its solvency, but even when investors know the rumors are unfounded, it may be in their individual interests to join the run, as few entities can remain solvent if their assets must be sold at fire-sale prices. Thus, fears of a run have the potential to become at least partially self-fulfilling, and a run may blur the distinction between an insolvent and an illiquid firm.

An increase in the risk of a run induces financial firms to hoard liquidity, for example, by shifting asset holdings into highly liquid securities such as Treasury securities. The supply of highly liquid securities being relatively inelastic in the short run, such efforts do not increase the liquidity of the financial system as a whole, but serve only to raise the price of liquid assets while reducing the market value of less-liquid assets such as loans. Liquidity pressures thus make firms less willing to extend credit to both financial and nonfinancial firms. Central banks, such as the Federal Reserve, can mitigate liquidity problems by lending against less-liquid but nevertheless sound collateral; indeed, serving as "lender of last resort" has been central banks' key weapon against financial panics for hundreds of years. However, the Federal Reserve under normal conditions is permitted to lend only to depository institutions and had the authority to lend to nondepositories only in unusual and exigent circumstances. Thus, the Federal Reserve could not directly address liquidity problems at nondepositories until the crisis was well underway.

Money market mutual funds proved particularly vulnerable to liquidity pressures. A large portion of the investments of these funds were in short-term wholesale funding instruments issued or guaranteed by commercial banks. When short-term wholesale funding markets came under stress, particularly in the period after the collapse of Lehman Brothers, money market mutual funds faced runs by their investors. Although actions by the Treasury and the Federal Reserve helped arrest these runs, the money market mutual funds responded by hoarding liquidity, thus constricting the availability of financing to financial and nonfinancial firms.

Currency mismatches also contributed to the disruption of wholesale funding patterns during the crisis. For example, major European financial institutions guaranteed the liabilities of some shadow banks. Some of them mainly bought dollar-denominated asset-backed securities and raised funding in the U.S. dollar commercial paper market. When these vehicles lost access to commercial paper funding, their bank guarantors sought dollar funding in dollar-denominated wholesale markets and foreign exchange swap markets. The heavy demand for dollars, coupled with investor concerns about the health of some European banks, put significant stress on these markets. This stress could not be alleviated by foreign monetary authorities through their normal operations, which provide liquidity in their own currencies but not in dollars. The Federal Reserve and other central banks addressed the problem by establishing dollar liquidity swap agreements.

Deficiencies in Risk Management

Although the vulnerabilities associated with short-term wholesale funding can be seen as a structural weakness of the global financial system, they can also be viewed as a consequence of poor risk management by issuers and investors Unfortunately, the crisis revealed many other significant defects in private-sector risk management and risk controls. Examples included a significant deterioration of mortgage underwriting standards before the crisis, which was not limited to subprime borrowers; a similar weakening of underwriting standards for commercial real estate loans, together with poor management of concentration risk and other risks by commercial real estate lenders; excessive reliance by investors on credit ratings, especially in the case of structured credit products; and insufficient capacity by many large firms to track firmwide risk exposures, including off-balance-sheet exposures. Among other problems, risk-management weaknesses led to inadequate risk diversification by major financial firms, so that losses--rather than being dispersed broadly among investors--proved in some cases to be heavily concentrated, threatening the stability of the affected companies. Risk-management weaknesses were spread throughout the financial system, including at many institutions that were neither large nor too-big-to-fail. For example, problems with commercial real estate lending were concentrated in regional and community banks. Subprime lending was done by small as well as large firms.

Private-sector risk management also failed to keep up with financial innovation in many cases. An important example is the extension of the traditional originate-to-distribute business model to encompass increasingly complex securitized credit products, with wholesale market funding playing a key role. In general, the originate-to-distribute model breaks down the process of credit extension into components or stages--from origination to financing and to the post-financing monitoring of the borrower's ability to repay--in a manner reminiscent of how contemporary manufacturers distribute the stages of production across firms and locations. This general approach has been used in various forms for many years and can produce significant benefits, including lower credit costs and increased access of small and medium-sized borrowers to the broader capital markets. However, the expanded use of this model to finance subprime mortgages through securitization was mismanaged at several points, including the initial underwriting, which deteriorated markedly in part because of incentive schemes that effectively rewarded originators for the quantity rather than the quality of the mortgages extended. Loans were then packaged into securities that proved complex and unwieldy; for example, when defaults became widespread, the legal agreements underlying the securitizations made reasonable modifications of troubled mortgages difficult. Rating agencies' ratings of asset-backed securities were revealed to be subject to conflicts of interest and faulty models. At the end of the chain were investors that often relied mainly on ratings. Even if the end-investors wanted to do their own credit analysis, the information needed to do so was often difficult or impossible to obtain.

Leverage

Excessive leverage is often cited as an important vulnerability that contributed to the crisis. Certainly, many households, businesses, and financial firms took on more debt than they could handle, reflecting in part more permissive standards on the part of lenders. A notable example was the decline in down payments required of many home purchasers, which, together with the increased use of exotic mortgage instruments and the availability of home equity lines of credit, resulted in some homeowners becoming highly leveraged. When house prices declined, the equity of those homeowners was quickly wiped out; in turn, "underwater" borrowers who owed more than their houses were worth were much more likely to default on their mortgage payments. Nonfinancial firms, in contrast, do not seem to have become overleveraged before the crisis; collectively, these firms did see a small increase in debt-to-asset ratios from 2006 to 2008, but these ratios tend to be volatile, and the short-term increase was superimposed on a two-decade-long downward trend.

Assessing trends in leverage for financial firms is not completely straightforward, in part because available statistics are inadequate and also because, in a world of complex financial instruments, leverage can be very difficult to measure. Traditional measures do not show a large increase in aggregate financial-sector leverage. At large U.S. commercial bank holding companies, for instance, equity capital relative to assets increased somewhat from 2001 through 2006. However, the quality of capital declined--for example, the share of intangible assets increased; consequently, in the crisis, true loss-absorbing capital was often much lower than accounting measures suggested. Moreover, many derivatives contracts have something similar to balance sheet leverage embedded in their structures, so that investors in derivatives can be more leveraged than their balance sheets imply. And, of course, some individual financial firms were overleveraged even by traditional measures.

Leverage tends to be procyclical--rising in good times, when the confidence of lenders and borrowers is high, and falling in bad times, when confidence turns to caution. This procyclicality increases financial and economic stress in the downturn. For example, the decline in required down payments on home purchases seen before the crisis has now sharply reversed, with required down payments of 20 or 30 percent of the house price becoming increasingly common. These tougher requirements, while understandable from the perspective of lenders, have reduced the pool of potential homebuyers. With fewer buyers, downward pressure on home prices increases. Lower house prices help to improve affordability but also weaken the financial positions of current homeowners, reducing their capacity to service their mortgages, to purchase new homes, and to consume goods and services.

Another procyclical pattern in leverage occurred in the financing practices of many financial firms. For example, recent academic studies have focused on the financing practices of hedge funds, securities broker-dealers, and other similar entities.[3] These entities' assets are primarily marketable securities, and much of their financing is in the form of repos. When times are good, the value of the assets rises and repo lenders impose smaller haircuts on the collateral, allowing more securities to be financed by a given amount of repo borrowing--effectively, an increase in leverage.[4] When times turn bad, the value of the assets falls and more-cautious repo lenders demand higher haircuts. In such a situation, the borrower's main available response is to sell assets. However, in the aggregate, such forced sales, particularly into illiquid markets, tend to amplify the downturn in asset values. Declines in asset prices, together with fears of further declines, tend to result in lenders demanding still higher haircuts, which forces more asset sales, and so on. Such phenomena were particularly important in the run-up to the acquisition of Bear Stearns in March 2008 and in the most intense phase of the crisis in September and October 2008.

Derivatives

Derivatives had a mixed record in the crisis. Throughout the period, virtually all derivatives contracts settled according to their terms, and there were few reported instances of bankruptcy or financial stress resulting from speculative use of interest rate, foreign exchange, commodity, or equity derivatives, which taken together form the vast majority of contracts

---

[3] See, for example, Markus Brunnermeier and Lasse Heje Pedersen (2009), "Market Liquidity and Funding Liquidity," *Review of Financial Studies*, vol. 27 (6), pp. 2201-38.

[4] A *haircut* is the amount of excess collateral required by the lender. For example, if the haircut is 10 percent, the borrower must post $1 of collateral for each 90 cents borrowed.

outstanding. In many cases, derivatives allowed financial and nonfinancial entities to better hedge their risks. However, some entities did use credit derivatives as a tool for taking excessive risks, most notably the insurance company American International Group (AIG). In that case, the problem was perhaps less the use of derivatives than a massive failure of risk management, especially by the parts of AIG that took large positions in credit derivatives. AIG neither hedged nor provided adequate capital against the large, correlated risks that it was taking. AIG's actions were facilitated by gaps in prudential regulation, as I will discuss. The consequences for the broader system were so severe because AIG was a large financial firm closely interlinked with other systemically important financial institutions and markets.

A useful distinction can be drawn between the derivatives instruments themselves and the infrastructure for clearing and settling derivatives instruments. For over-the-counter derivatives, the clearing and settlement infrastructure was seriously inadequate. This point was recognized before the crisis; the Federal Reserve made some progress through voluntary cooperation with the industry and other regulators.[5]

At times, the complexity and diversity of derivatives instruments also posed problems. Financial firms sometimes found it quite difficult to fully assess their own net derivatives exposures or to communicate to counterparties and regulators the nature and extent of those exposures. The associated uncertainties helped fuel losses of confidence that contributed importantly to the liquidity problems I mentioned earlier. The recent legislation addresses these issues by requiring that derivatives contracts be traded on exchanges or other regulated trading facilities when possible and that they be centrally cleared. The legislation also requires stronger

---

[5] The Federal Reserve Bank of New York hosted a meeting in September 2005 with representatives of major market participants and their domestic and international supervisors to discuss a range of issued regarding the processing of over-the-counter derivatives. See Federal Reserve Bank of New York (2005), "Statement Regarding Meeting on Credit Derivatives," press release, September 15, www.newyorkfed.org/newsevents/news_archive/markets/2005/an050915.html.

prudential standards for financial firms that use derivatives and clearinghouses. These changes should increase the quality and availability of information, though measuring exposure is likely to continue to be a challenge.

Vulnerabilities and Shortfalls in the Public Sector

The vulnerabilities of the private sector amplified the triggers of the crisis, creating stresses and uncertainties that posed grave threats to financial and economic stability. The public sector also had important vulnerabilities, which exacerbated the crisis and made the public-sector response less effective than it should have been, both in the United States and in other countries. These vulnerabilities included both gaps in the statutory framework and flaws in the performance of regulators and supervisors.

Statutory Gaps and Conflicts

The statutory framework of financial regulation that was in place before the crisis contained serious gaps.

Critically, shadow banks were, for the most part, not subject to consistent and effective regulatory oversight. Many types of shadow banks lacked meaningful prudential regulation, including various special purpose vehicles (such as CLOs), ABCP vehicles, hedge funds, and many nonbank mortgage-origination companies. No regulatory body restricted the leverage and liquidity policies of these entities, and few if any regulatory standards were imposed on the quality of their risk management or the prudence of their risk-taking. Market discipline, imposed by creditors and counterparties, helped on some dimensions but did not effectively limit systemic risks these entities posed. Of these shadow banks, both special purpose vehicles and nonbank mortgage originators contributed significantly to the crisis; hedge funds, which were often cited as a potential systemic risk before the crisis, generally did not, perhaps because the concerns about them meant they were subject to more-effective market discipline.

Other shadow banks were potentially subject to some prudential oversight, but weaknesses in the statutory and regulatory framework meant that in practice they were inadequately regulated and supervised. For example, the Securities and Exchange Commission (SEC) regulated broker-dealer holding companies but only through an opt-in arrangement that lacked the force of a statutory regulatory regime. Large broker-dealer holding companies faced serious losses and funding problems during the crisis, and the instability of such firms as Bear Stearns and Lehman Brothers severely damaged the financial system. Similarly, AIG's insurance operations were supervised and regulated by various state and international insurance regulators, and the Office of Thrift Supervision technically had authority to supervise AIG as a thrift holding company. However, oversight of AIG Financial Products, which housed the derivatives activities that imposed major losses on the firm, was extremely limited in practice.

A lack of statutory authority carried with it a lack of information. Shadow banks that were unregulated were not required to report data that would adequately reveal their risk positions or practices. Moreover, the lack of preexisting reporting and supervisory relationships hindered systematic gathering of information that might have helped in the early days of the crisis.

A broader failing was that, for historical reasons, regulation and supervision were focused on the safety and soundness (or the practices) of individual financial institutions or markets. However, in the United States and most other advanced economies, no governmental entity had sufficient authority--now often called macroprudential authority--to take actions to limit systemic risks. For example, most ABCP vehicles were small relative to the size of the sponsoring bank.

Had the Federal Reserve or another regulator attempted to shut down or restrict these vehicles, sponsoring banks could have argued (quite correctly) that, individually, these vehicles were too small to threaten the safety and soundness of their sponsoring institutions. But many small vehicles, and a few big ones, that were spread across a lot of banks added up to a systemic vulnerability. This example also highlights the importance of international cooperation in a globally connected system. U.S. action to more tightly regulate such vehicles would have been ineffective unless foreign regulators had taken similar actions, as many of the vehicles were sponsored by financial institutions overseas.

The partitioning of authority that characterized bank supervision and regulation in the United States before the crisis amounted to another statutory gap, or at least a gray area in the law. The Gramm-Leach-Bliley Act required the Federal Reserve in its supervision of bank holding companies to defer to the primary supervisor of functionally regulated subsidiaries as much as possible, a system often referred to as "Fed-lite." For example, the Fed was required to defer to the Office of the Comptroller of the Currency (OCC) in the case of national bank subsidiaries, and to the SEC for broker-dealer subsidiaries. Although the agencies shared information and their cooperation was cordial, in practice the Gramm-Leach-Bliley requirements made it difficult for any single regulator to reliably see the whole picture of the activities and risks of large, complex banking institutions.

Some of the most significant and costly problems arose in the government-sponsored enterprises related to housing, Fannie Mae and Freddie Mac. Although these two companies were subject to regulatory oversight, the statutory framework for that oversight was problematic. Fannie and Freddie were nominally private corporations, but they enjoyed cost advantages from the implicit federal guarantee on their liabilities; these cost advantages allowed them to act as a duopoly in a number of businesses, including providing credit guarantees and securitizing conforming mortgages. Their securities were exempt from a number of SEC registration and reporting requirements. Until mid-2008, their prudential regulator was the Office of Federal Housing Enterprise Oversight (OFHEO) within the Department of Housing and Urban Development, which had a dual--and sometimes conflicting--mission of promoting homeownership and preserving the safety and soundness of Fannie and Freddie. As a practical matter, the dual mission made it more difficult for OFHEO to promote safety and soundness if its actions might limit the volume of mortgage originations. Fannie and Freddie were permitted to operate with capital that was both of low quality and of inadequate size to buffer the risks in their portfolios. In addition, their balance sheets were allowed to grow rapidly, including through purchases of subprime mortgage-backed securities.

Many of these statutory gaps have been addressed by the recently passed financial reform legislation. Notably, the establishment of a Financial Stability Oversight Council, together with new authorities for regulators, should increase the macroprudential orientation of regulation and supervision. Under the new legislation, all systemically critical financial institutions, including those that are not bank holding companies, will be subject to consolidated supervision; additionally, the Gramm-Leach-Bliley restrictions have been modified to allow the Federal Reserve to gain a more comprehensive view of large financial companies.

Ineffective Use of Existing Authorities

Statutory gaps were an important reason for the buildup of risk in the system and for the inadequate response of the public sector to that buildup. But even when authorities did exist, they were not always used forcefully or effectively enough by regulators and supervisors. I will give a few examples of flaws in execution by U.S. bank regulators because I am most familiar with them, but I want to note that, with the benefit of hindsight, many financial regulators around the world fell short on various dimensions.[6]

For the most part, bank regulators did not do enough to force large financial institutions to strengthen their internal risk-management systems or to curtail risky practices. For example, the Federal Reserve's supervisory capital assessment program (SCAP), popularly known as the "stress tests," demonstrated that many institutions' information systems could not provide timely, accurate information about bank exposures to counterparties nor complete information about the risks posed by different positions and portfolios. Regulators had recognized these problems in some cases but did not press firms vigorously enough to fix them. The SCAP also revealed inadequacies in many banks' internal capital assessment methods that might have been recognized earlier.

A number of triggers of the crisis were linked to deficiencies in the protection of consumers in the financial marketplace, notably in subprime mortgage lending. The Federal Reserve addressed a number of these issues prior to the crisis through guidance to banking organizations and through enforcement, and in the past three years or so the Fed has issued strong regulations to protect consumers in a number of key areas, including mortgages, credit cards, and debit cards. However, in the period before the crisis, the Fed was slow to identify and address abuses in subprime lending, especially those outside the banking firms that the Fed regulates directly.

Although the absence of macroprudential authorities was an important statutory gap, regulators could have done more to try to identify risks to the broader financial system. In

---

[6] My colleagues on the Board of Governors and I have discussed these issues and our responses in more detail in various testimonies and speeches. See, for example, my testimony on March 17, 2010, before the House Financial Services Committee, "The Federal Reserve's Role in Bank Supervision," www.federalreserve.gov/newsevents/testimony/bernanke20100317a.htm.

retrospect, stronger bank capital standards--notably those relating to the quality of capital and the amount of capital required for banks' trading book assets--and more attention to the liquidity risks faced by banks and other financial institutions would have made the financial system as a whole more resilient.

For its part, the Federal Reserve has moved vigorously to address identified problems. On the regulatory side, we are playing a key role in ongoing international efforts to ensure that systemically critical financial institutions hold more and higher-quality capital, have enough liquidity to survive highly stressed conditions, and meet demanding standards for company-wide risk management. We also addressed flawed compensation practices by issuing guidance to help ensure that compensation structures at banking organizations provide appropriate incentives without encouraging excessive risk-taking.[7]

To improve both our consolidated supervision and our ability to identify potential risks to the financial system, we have made substantial changes to our supervisory framework. So that we can better understand linkages among firms and markets that have the potential to undermine the stability of the financial system, we have adopted a more explicitly multidisciplinary approach, making use of the Federal Reserve's broad expertise in economics, financial markets, payment systems, and bank supervision. We are also augmenting our traditional supervisory approach that focuses on firm-by-firm examinations with greater use of horizontal reviews that look across a group of firms to identify common sources of risks and best practices for managing those risks. To supplement information from examiners in the field, we have begun an enhanced quantitative surveillance program for large bank holding companies that will use data analysis

---

[7] For additional information, see Board of Governors of the Federal Reserve System (2009), "Federal Reserve Issues Proposed Guidance on Incentive Compensation," press release, October 22, www.federalreserve.gov/newsevents/press/bcreg/20091022a.htm; also see Board of Governors of the Federal Reserve System (2010), "Federal Reserve, OCC, OTS, FDIC Issue Final Guidance on Incentive Compensation," press release, June 21, www.federalreserve.gov/newsevents/press/bcreg/20100621a.htm.

and formal modeling to help identify vulnerabilities at both the firm level and for the financial sector as a whole. This analysis will be supported by the collection of more timely, detailed, and consistent data from regulated firms. Many of these changes draw on the lessons provided by the SCAP.

Improvements in the supervisory framework will lead to better outcomes only if day-to-day supervision is well executed, with risks identified early and promptly remediated. To facilitate swifter, more-effective supervisory responses, we have increased the degree of centralization of the oversight and control of our supervisory function, with shared accountability by senior Board and Reserve Bank supervisory staff and active oversight by the Board of Governors. Supervisory concerns will be communicated to firms promptly and at a high level, with more-frequent involvement of senior bank managers and boards of directors and senior Federal Reserve officials. Where necessary, we will increase the use of formal and informal enforcement actions to ensure prompt and effective remediation of serious issues.

Crisis-Management Capabilities

Once a crisis occurs, timely and effective action by the government is critical to containing the severity of financial disruptions and their economic effects. Ultimately, financial stability was regained through congressional action to recapitalize the banking system, the provision of liquidity by the Federal Reserve and of debt and deposit guarantees by the Federal Deposit Insurance Corporation (FDIC), and important actions by the Treasury Department. However, the crisis revealed large gaps in the government's ability to respond quickly, effectively, and with minimum cost to taxpayers and the economy.

Crucially, in contrast to the regime in place for depository organizations, no one in the U.S. government had legal authority to resolve failing nonbank financial institutions, including bank holding companies, in a way that would impose appropriate losses on creditors while limiting systemic effects. Especially during the short time frames required by a crisis, Chapter 11 bankruptcy, which focuses on creditor rights rather than on financial and economic stability, is not an effective vehicle for managing the liquidation or restructuring of large, complex, and highly interconnected financial institutions. The failure of Lehman Brothers through Chapter 11 proceedings worsened the crisis enormously. Loans were made to AIG because a bankruptcy filing by that company would have redoubled the severity of the crisis.

The creation of a resolution regime for systemically critical nonbank financial firms is a critical innovation of the recently passed financial reform bill. Work is under way to implement this framework. Supervisors are also working to address other resolution-related challenges that policymakers faced during the crisis, including unnecessarily complex corporate structures at many financial institutions and complications arising from the global nature of operations of many large financial institutions.

In a time of panic and liquidity shortages, central banks must be able to provide funding to sound financial institutions. In the United States, the Federal Reserve lacked established procedures to provide short-term funding to shadow banks, such as broker-dealers, money market mutual funds, or special purpose vehicles, so it had to develop programs to provide such funding quickly during the crisis. The Federal Reserve had the authority to lend to depository institutions through the discount window; however, to a surprising extent, banks were reluctant to use the window, even when they had pressing needs for funding. This reluctance arose from the "stigma" of using the window; each bank feared that if it went to the window and markets learned they had done so, such action would be interpreted as a sign of weakness, and their funding problems would worsen rather than improve.

However, the Federal Reserve was able to supply liquidity to both banks and nonbanks, through a variety of means, to stem the panic. It auctioned fixed amounts of term funding to depository institutions, which seemed to circumvent the stigma problem. The Federal Reserve also created other facilities, in most cases using its emergency authority under section 13(3) of the Federal Reserve Act, to provide collateralized short-term loans to nonbank financial institutions in situations in which market-based funding mechanisms had broken down.

"Too Big to Fail"

Many of the vulnerabilities that amplified the crisis are linked with the problem of so-called too-big-to-fail firms. A too-big-to-fail firm is one whose size, complexity, interconnectedness, and critical functions are such that, should the firm go unexpectedly into liquidation, the rest of the financial system and the economy would face severe adverse consequences. Governments provide support to too-big-to-fail firms in a crisis not out of favoritism or particular concern for the management, owners, or creditors of the firm, but because they recognize that the consequences for the broader economy of allowing a disorderly failure greatly outweigh the costs of avoiding the failure in some way. Common means of avoiding failure include facilitating a merger, providing credit, or injecting government capital, all of which protect at least some creditors who otherwise would have suffered losses.

In the midst of the crisis, providing support to a too-big-to-fail firm usually represents the best of bad alternatives; without such support there could be substantial damage to the economy. However, the existence of too-big-to-fail firms creates several problems in the long run.

First, too-big-to-fail generates a severe moral hazard. If creditors believe that an institution will not be allowed to fail, they will not demand as much compensation for risks as they otherwise would, thus weakening market discipline; nor will they invest as many resources in monitoring the firm's risk-taking. As a result, too-big-to-fail firms will tend to take more risk than desirable, in the expectation that they will receive assistance if their bets go bad. Where they have the necessary authority, regulators will try to limit that risk-taking, but without the help of market discipline they will find it difficult to do so, even if authorities are nominally sufficient. The buildup of risk in too-big-to-fail firms increases the possibility of a financial crisis and worsens the crisis when it occurs. There is little doubt that excessive risk-taking by too-big-to-fail firms significantly contributed to the crisis, with Fannie Mae and Freddie Mac being prominent examples.

A second cost of too-big-to-fail is that it creates an uneven playing field between big and small firms. This unfair competition, together with the incentive to grow that too-big-to-fail provides, increases risk and artificially raises the market share of too-big-to-fail firms, to the detriment of economic efficiency as well as financial stability.

Third, as we saw in 2008 and 2009, too-big-to-fail firms can themselves become major risks to overall financial stability, particularly in the absence of adequate resolution tools. The failure of Lehman Brothers and the near-failure of several other large, complex firms significantly worsened the crisis and the recession by disrupting financial markets, impeding credit flows, inducing sharp declines in asset prices, and hurting confidence. The failures of smaller, less interconnected firms, though certainly of significant concern, have not had substantial effects on the stability of the financial system as a whole.

If the crisis has a single lesson, it is that the too-big-to-fail problem must be solved. Simple declarations that the government will not assist firms in the future, or restrictions that make providing assistance more difficult, will not be credible on their own. Few governments will accept devastating economic costs if a rescue can be conducted at a lesser cost; even if one

Administration refrained from rescuing a large, complex firm, market participants would believe that others might not refrain in the future. Thus, a promise not to intervene in and of itself will not solve the problem.

The new financial reform law and current negotiations on new Basel capital and liquidity regulations have together set into motion a three-part strategy to address too-big-to-fail. First, the propensity for excessive risk-taking by large, complex, interconnected firms must be greatly reduced. Among the tools that will be used to achieve this goal are more-rigorous capital and liquidity requirements, including higher standards for systemically critical firms; tougher regulation and supervision of the largest firms, including restrictions on activities and on the structure of compensation packages; and measures to increase transparency and market discipline. Oversight of the largest firms must take into account not only their own safety and soundness, but also the systemic risks they pose.

Second, as I already discussed, a resolution regime is being implemented that allows the government to resolve a distressed, systemically important financial firm in a fashion that avoids disorderly liquidation while imposing losses on creditors and shareholders. Ensuring that that new regime is workable and credible will be a critical challenge for regulators.

Finally, the more resilient the financial system, the less the cost of a failure of a large firm, and thus the less incentive the government has to prevent that failure. Examples of policies to increase resiliency include the requirements in the recent bill to force more derivatives settlement into clearinghouses and to strengthen the prudential oversight of key financial market utilities such as clearinghouses and exchanges. Even if such steps do not meaningfully affect investor perceptions about too-big-to-fail, they are worthwhile in that they will reduce the vulnerability of the financial system to future shocks. In addition, prudential regulators should take actions to reduce systemic risks. Examples include requiring firms to have less-complex corporate structures that make effective resolution of a failing firm easier, and requiring clearing and settlement procedures that reduce vulnerable interconnections among firms.

Monetary Policy and Related Factors

Some have argued that monetary policy contributed significantly to the bubble in housing prices, which in turn was a trigger of the crisis. The question is a complex one, with ramifications for future policy that are still under debate; I will comment on the issue only briefly.

The Federal Open Market Committee brought short-term interest rates to a very low level during and following the 2001 recession, in response to persistent sluggishness in the labor market and what at the time was perceived as a potential risk of deflation. Those actions were in accord with the FOMC's mandate from the Congress to promote maximum employment and price stability; indeed, the labor market recovered from that episode and price stability was maintained.

Did the low level of short-term interest rates undertaken for the purposes of macroeconomic stabilization inadvertently make a significant contribution to the housing bubble? It is frankly quite difficult to determine the causes of booms and busts in asset prices; psychological phenomena are no doubt important, as argued by Robert Shiller, for example.[8] However, studies of the empirical linkage between monetary policy and house prices have generally found that that that linkage is much weaker than would be needed to explain the

---

[8] See Robert J. Shiller (2005), *Irrational Exuberance*, 2nd ed. (Princeton, N.J.: Princeton University Press); and George Akerlof and Robert J. Shiller (2009), *Animal Spirits: How Human Psychology Drives the Economy and Why It Matters for Global Capitalism* (Princeton, N.J.: Princeton University Press).

behavior of house prices in terms of FOMC policies during this period.[9] Cross-national evidence also does not favor this hypothesis. For example, as documented by the International Monetary Fund, even though some countries other than the United States had substantial booms in house prices, there was little correlation across industrial countries between measures of monetary tightness or ease and changes in house prices.[10] For example, the United Kingdom also experienced a major boom and bust in house prices during the 2000s, but the Bank of England's policy rate went below 4 percent for only a few months in 2003.

The evidence is more consistent with a view that the run-up in house prices primarily represented a feedback loop between optimism regarding house prices and developments in the mortgage market. In mortgage markets, a combination of financial innovations and the vulnerabilities I mentioned earlier led to the extension of mortgages on increasingly easy terms to less-qualified borrowers, driving up the effective demand for housing and raising prices. Rising prices in turn further fueled optimism about the housing market and further increased the willingness of lenders to further weaken mortgage terms. Importantly, innovations in mortgage lending and the easing of standards had far greater effects on borrowers' monthly payments and housing affordability than did changes in monetary policy.[11]

The high rate of foreign investment in the United States also likely played a role in the housing boom. For many years, the United States has run large trade deficits while some

---

[9] For example, see Jane Dokko, Brian Doyle, Michael T. Kiley, Jinill Kim, Shane Sherlund, Jae Sim, and Skander Van den Heuvel (2009), "Monetary Policy and the Housing Bubble," Finance and Economics Discussion Series 2009-49 (Washington: Board of Governors of the Federal Reserve System, December), available at www.federalreserve.gov/PUBS/FEDS/2009/200949; Edward L. Glaeser, Stuart S. Rosenthal, and William C. Strange (2010) "Can Cheap Credit Explain the Housing Boom?" working paper (Cambridge, Mass.: Harvard University, July); and Charles Bean, Matthias Paustian, Adrian Penalver, and Tim Taylor (2010), "Monetary Policy after the Fall," paper presented at a symposium sponsored by the Federal Reserve Bank of Kansas City, held in Jackson Hole, Wyo., August 28.

[10] See International Monetary Fund (2009), *World Economic Outlook: Sustaining the Recovery*, chapter 3 (Washington: IMF, October).

[11] See Dokko and others, "Monetary Policy and the Housing Bubble," in note 9.

emerging-market economies, notably some Asian nations and some oil producers, have run large trade surpluses. Such a trade pattern is necessarily coupled with financial flows from the surplus to the deficit countries. International investment position statistics show that the excess savings of Asian nations have predominantly been put into U.S. government and agency debt and mortgage-backed securities, which would tend to lower real long-term interest rates, including mortgage rates. In international comparisons, there appears to be a strong connection between house price booms and significant capital inflows, in contrast to the aforementioned weak relationship found between monetary policy and house prices.[12]

International investment position statistics show that the United States also received significant capital inflows from Europe in the years before the crisis. Europe's trade has been about balanced over the past decade or so, implying no large net capital flows on average. However, substantial gross flows occurred in the years running up to the crisis. Notably, European institutions issued large amounts of debt in the United States, using the proceeds to buy private-sector debt, including securitized products. On balance, the effect of these sales and purchases on Europe's capital account balance approximately netted out, but the combination led to growing European exposures to the kind of distress in U.S. private-sector debt markets that occurred during the crisis. The strength of the demand for U.S. private structured debt products by European and other foreign investors likely helped to maintain downward pressure on U.S. credit spreads, thereby reducing the costs that risky borrowers paid and thus, all else being equal, increasing their demand for loans.

---

[12] See IMF, *World Economic Outlook*, in note 10; also see Alan G. Ahearne, John Ammer, Brian M. Doyle, Linda S. Kole, and Robert F. Martin (2005), "Monetary Policy and Housing Prices: A Cross-Country Study," International Finance Discussion Papers 2005-841 (Washington: Federal Reserve Board of Governors, September), available at www.federalreserve.gov/Pubs/IFDP/2005/841/default.htm.

Even if monetary policy was not a principal cause of the housing bubble, some have argued that the Fed could have stopped the bubble at an earlier stage by more-aggressive interest rate increases. For several reasons, this was not a practical policy option. First, in 2003 or so, when the policy rate was at its lowest level, there was little agreement about whether the increase in housing prices was a bubble or not (or, a popular hypothesis, that there was a bubble but that it was restricted to certain parts of the country). Second, and more important, monetary policy is a blunt tool; raising the general level of interest rates to manage a single asset price would undoubtedly have had large side effects on other assets and sectors of the economy. In this case, to significantly affect monthly payments and other measures of housing affordability, the FOMC likely would have had to increase interest rates quite sharply, at a time when the recovery was viewed as "jobless" and deflation was perceived as a threat.

A different line of argument holds that, by contributing to the long period of relatively placid economic and financial conditions sometimes known as the Great Moderation, monetary policy helped induce excessive complacency and insufficient attention to risk. Even though the two decades before the recent crisis included two recessions and several financial crises, including the bursting of the dot-com bubble, there may be some truth to this claim. However, it hardly follows that, in order to reduce risk-taking in financial markets, the Federal Reserve should impose the costs of instability on the entire economy.

Generally, financial regulation and supervision, rather than monetary policy, provide more-targeted tools for addressing credit-related problems. Enhancing financial stability through regulation and supervision leaves monetary policy free to focus on stability in growth and inflation, for which it is better suited. We should not categorically rule out using monetary policy to address financial imbalances, given the damage that they can cause; the FOMC is closely monitoring financial conditions for signs of such imbalances and will continue to do so. However, whenever possible, supervision and regulation should be the first line of defense against potential threats to financial stability.

Conclusion

The findings of this Commission will help us better understand the causes of the crisis, which in turn should increase our ability to avoid future crises and to mitigate the effects of crises that occur. We should not imagine, though, that it is possible to prevent all crises. A growing, dynamic economy requires a financial system that makes effective use of available saving in allocating credit to households and businesses. The provision of credit inevitably involves risk-taking. To achieve both sustained growth and stability, we need to provide a framework which promotes the appropriate mix of prudence, risk-taking, and innovation in our financial system.